Dedication
to my Mother Beverly Shaw
and the round table of inspiration

Children In the Military
Sylvan Crest Publishing
Box 2940
Mt. Vernon, ME. 04352

Copyright 1994 by Bonnie S. Linder. All rights reserved.
Printed in U.S.A.

No part of this series may be copied or reproduced without written permission from the publisher.
Children in the Military is a trademark of Sylvan Crest Publishing.

Library of Congress Cataloging-in-Publication Data–
Linder, Bonnie Shaw / Editor: Lockhart, Byron E.
On My Way / Dealing with a move
First edition / Mt. Vernon, ME.
Children in the Military / Library of Congress #94-92235

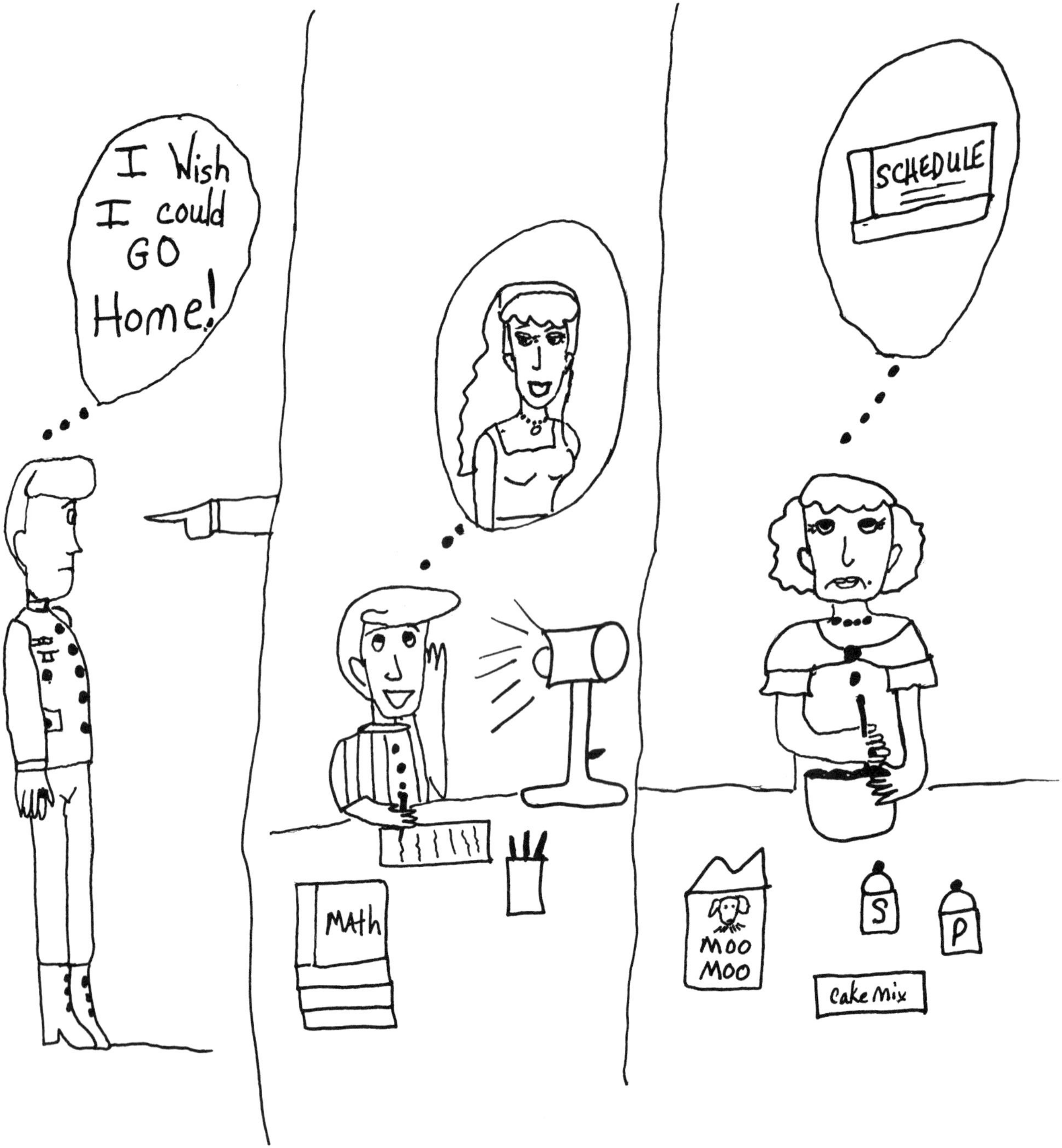
I Wish I could GO Home!
SCHEDULE
MATh
MOO MOO
S
P
cake Mix

Hi. My name is Janie and my Dad has to change duty stations. For Dad it means a new job. For Mom it means a new schedule. For my brother it probably means a new girlfriend. I'm not sure what it means for me.

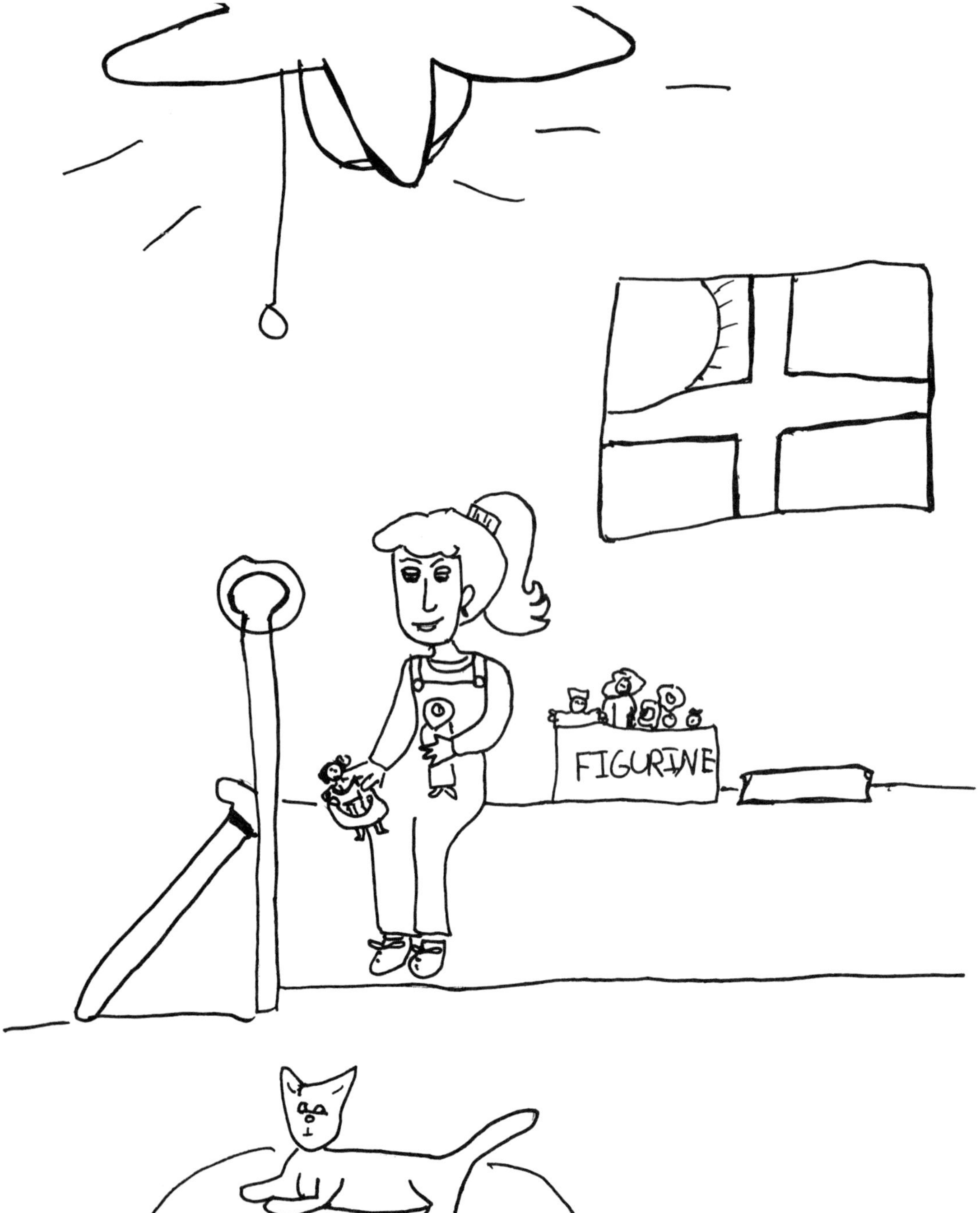
FIGURINE

The packers are coming. Mom says they're real careful, but I'm worried about my figurine collection. It's very fragile, and I would be sad if one broke.

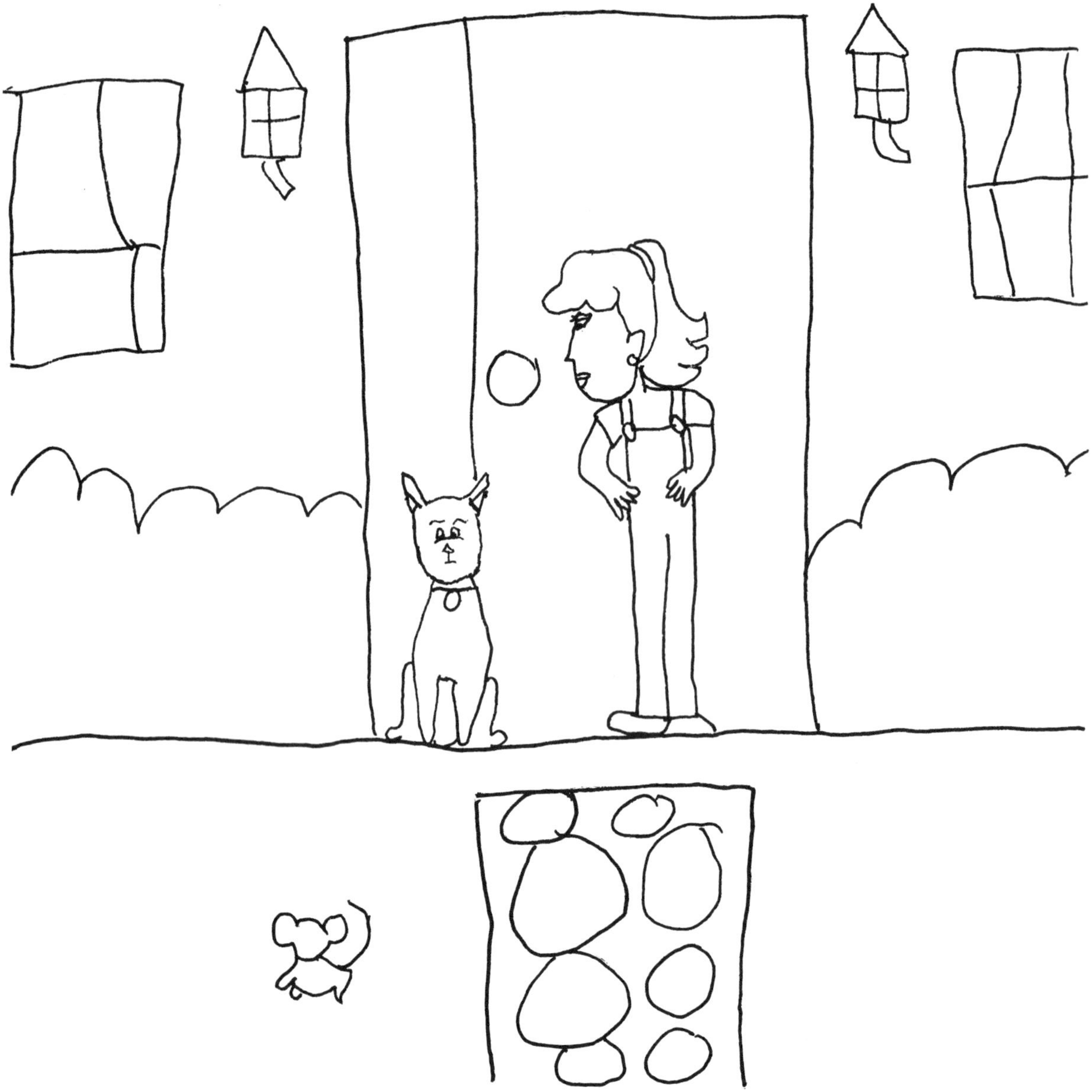

I think my cat Jasper knows that we're going too. She's following me everywhere, and not even trying to escape out the front door.

Everyone has an important job tomorrow. Dad is going to change the oil in the truck. Mom is going to clean stuff. My brother will write out the change of address cards. I'm supposed to keep an eye on Jasper to make sure she doesn't jump into a box by mistake. (Jasper loves boxes.) Mom says if Jasper gets in a box unnoticed she could starve on the trip. So my job is the most important.

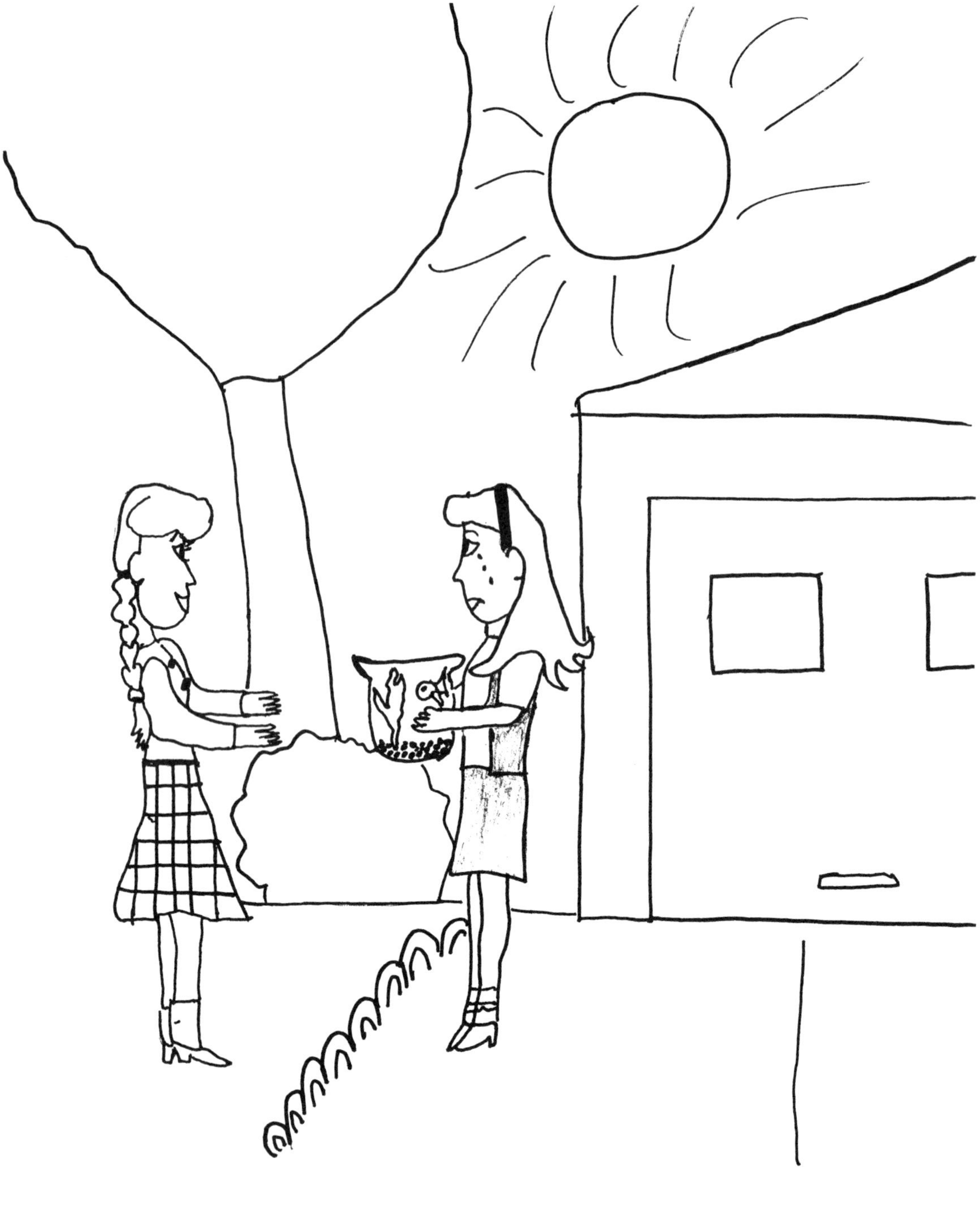

I had a goldfish named Lilly, but I had to give her to my best friend Kate. Dad said Lilly might not be strong enough to survive a big move. For a little while I wished I could move in with Kate too. I wasn't sure I was strong enough to leave my friends and start over in a new school.

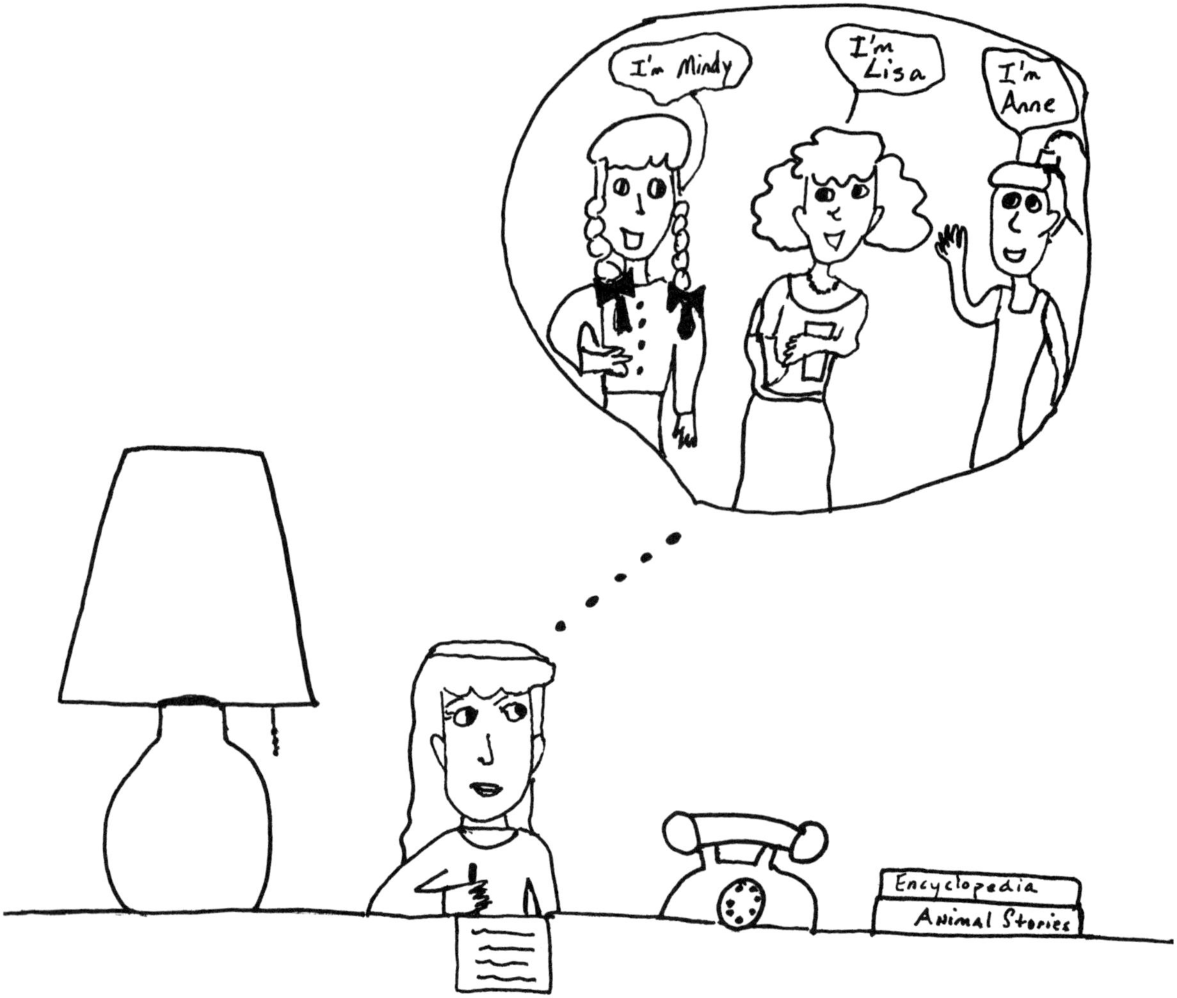

I'm Mindy
I'm Lisa
I'm Anne
Encyclopedia
Animal Stories

When I told my Mom, she asked me if I would like to have a pen pal to write to in my new school. I thought that sounded cool, so Mom wrote to the principal of my new school, and I ended up with three pen pals! I can hardly wait to meet my new friends that I've been writing to. I feel stronger knowing that there are some kids in my new class that already know me. I'll miss Kate a lot, but after I move, she will be my new pen pal.

Dear Janie,
I will miss
you when you
leave to go
But you'll
be happy in the
new school,
Miss Turner

ERASER

Last week I started a collection box. I've got some rocks, and pine cones, a nest, and some feathers from the trail near our house. My teacher gave me some things from school. An eraser, a pencil, and a note from her for luck. Anytime I feel lonesome for my home I can go through my collection. My brother says it's just a bunch of junk, but he's wrong.

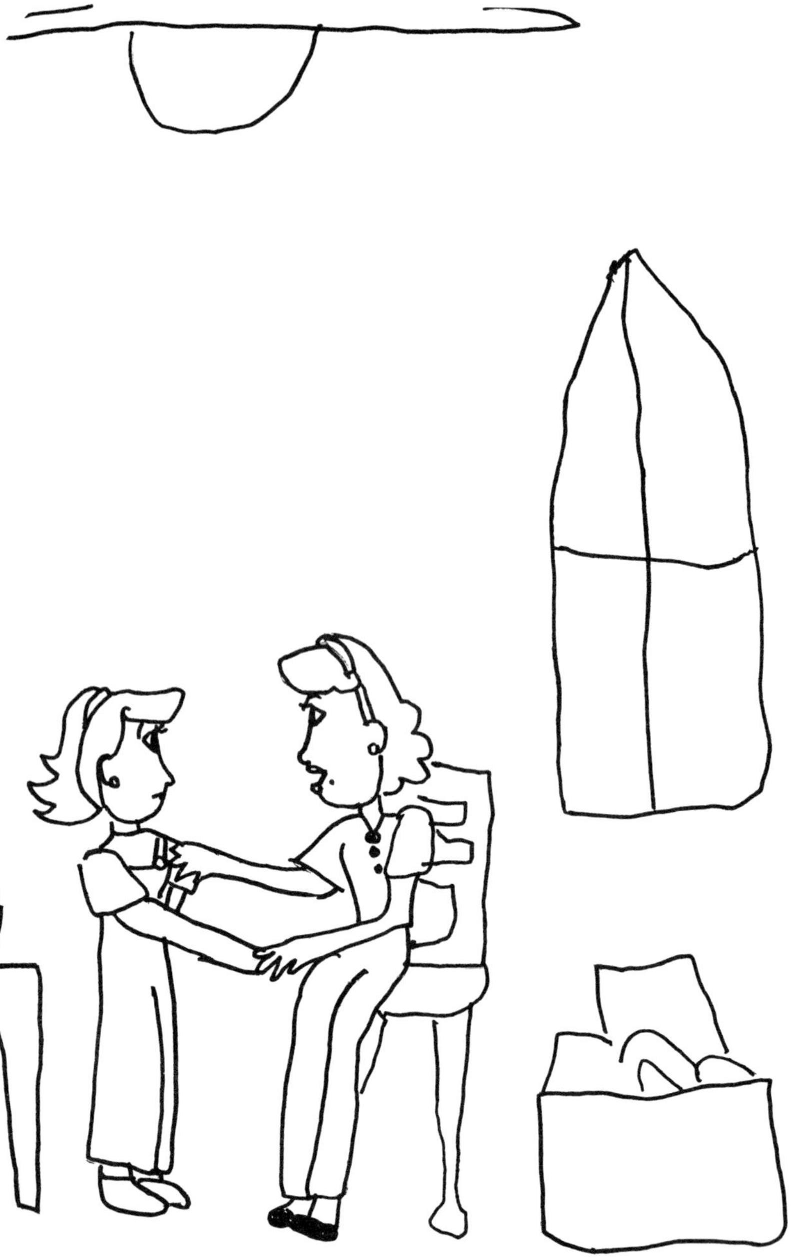

Part of me is sad about moving, but part of me is excited too. Dad says change is good. He says it makes us stronger. Mom says, "there is a purpose for everything," and we should, "bloom wherever we're planted."

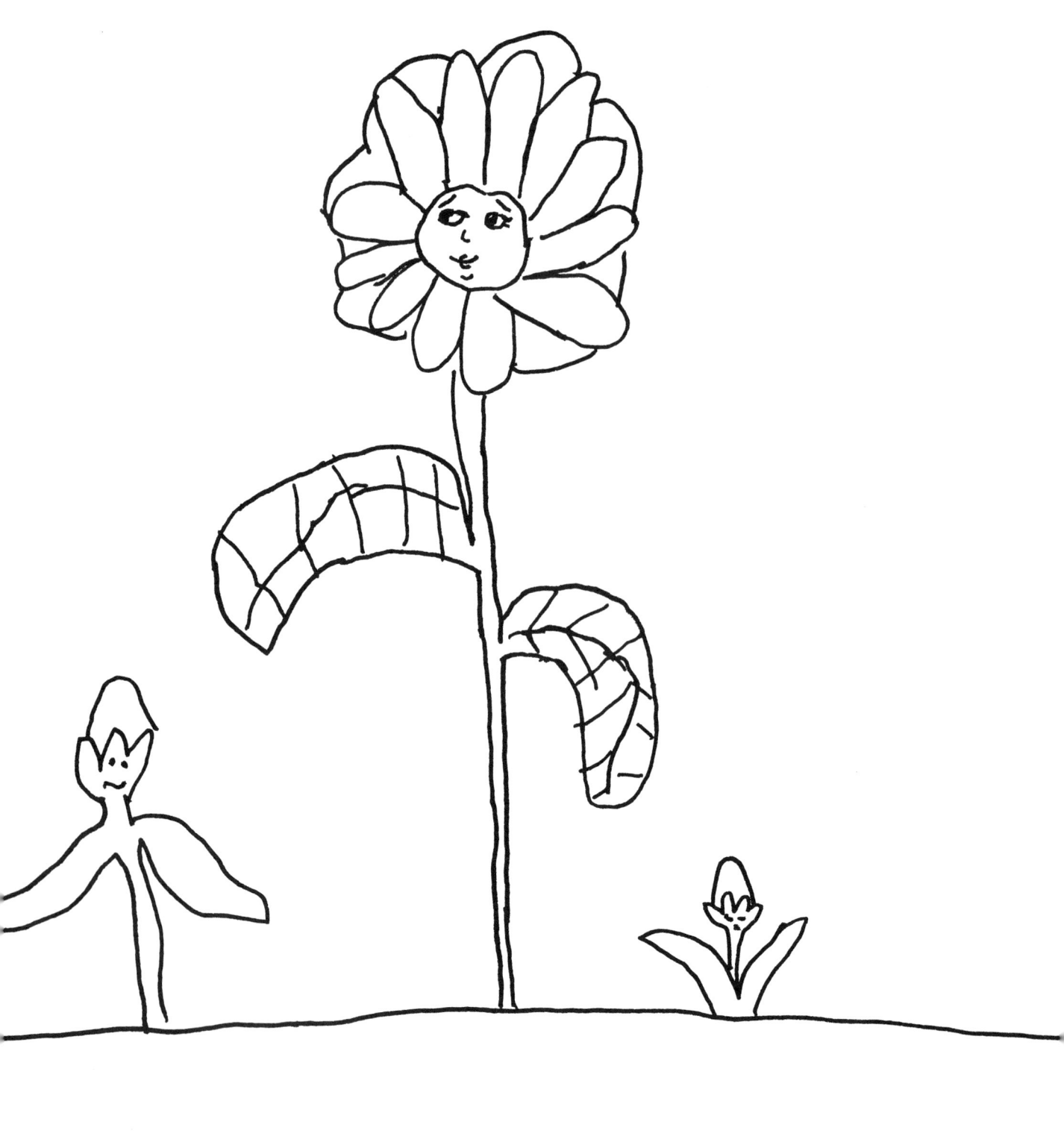

I asked her what that means and she said that we are like little seeds. When a seed is planted it sometimes dries up. But a good, healthy seed will grow into a lovely flower. Mom says I am a good, healthy seed so I should grow strong and blossom wherever I live. Then she gave me a big hug that made me feel very much at home.

I guess that's the answer. My family is my home, not the house we live in. So as long as those big hugs are there for me I can grow, and bloom, and maybe even shine!

ORDER FORM

Please send

_____ copies of <u>On My Way</u> at $4.95 each $ _____

Sales tax (sales tax in state of Maine,
add 6% or 30¢/book) $_____

Shipping-add $1.50/book $_____

Total $_____

Send check or money order payable to:
Sylvan Crest Publishing
RR 1 Box 2940
Mt. Vernon, ME.
04352

For inquiries regarding discounts on large orders call (207) 293-2058

Name _____

Organization _____

Address _____

_____

Telephone _____